Diet recommendations for TCM - Heart - Qi deficiency

Please check these recommendations always with a TCM nutrition consultant, therapist, doctor or dietician. The recipes and the list of ingredients are supporting also the conventional medical therapy. The calorie disclosures of fresh ingredients (fruit and vegetables) vary according to quality and time of harvest. The contents were checked by a dietician and a nutrition consultant for the Traditional Chinese Medicine (TCM).

Author:
©2017 Josef Miligui
www.ebns.at

AF220115

Source:
The lists are created from the EBNS database for nutritional counseling. The database is used by dietitians, therapists and doctors for advising the patient / client.

Literature:
The specialist literature and the training documents of the German and Austrian dietary and traditional Chinese medicine serve as a knowledge base. We have used the documents as a basis of knowledge, adapted it to our experience and completed them.
http://di-book.com

Title Photo:
©2008 Erika Weixlbaumer

Production and publishing:
BoD – Books on Demand, Norderstedt
ISBN: 9783752862263

Diet recommendations for TCM - Heart - Qi deficiency

1 Treatment strategy

Strengthen the heart qi (build up the spleen and kidneys via qi, activation of the qi and blood flow), blood buildup, as heart qi and heart blood deficiency cause each other. - hot LITTLE, cold NO, all other YES (only sour-refreshing and bitter-warm LITTLE)

2 Avoid

n.a.

3 Breakfast

	kkal. per serving
Beef broth	124
Coconut rice with cardamom	266
Fish soup with white wine, laurel and marjoram	199
Hummus (Chickpeasmash)	542
Legumes	31
Millet with egg and butter	338
Pea dish	406
Polenta with fried egg	410
Porridge with raisins and sake	427
Quinoa piquant with avocado	561
Quinoa with peach	247
Reissue soup with fresh fruits	143
Rice congee with carrots and fennel	131
Rice congee with dried fruit	210
Rice dulse soup	190
Rice noodle soup with shiitake mushrooms	65
Roasted oatmeal with grapes compote	328
Spelled-grid porridge with berries of the season	243
Sweet polenta with peach	330
Tea from ginseng	0
Tea from juniper berry	10
Warming porridge	357

4   Snack

5   Lunch

6   Afternoon

7   Dinner

8   Any time

9 Recipes

(recommendable) = You can use more.
(little) = You should use less than specified or omit.

9.1 8 treasures of rice

Strengthens kidney and bladder, builds up Qi, strengthens the spleen, repels moisture, reduces internal heat, prevents cancer, builds heart, calms nerves.
Cooking time approx. 1 hour
Calories p. portion: 212
4 portions

Quantity of ingredients
Lily bulbs 1 table spoon / 5g. (recommended)................................. *
Longane 1 table spoon / 5g. (recommended)................................. *
King Solomon's-seal 1 table spoon / 5g. (recommended)................. *
Yam root, yam root tuber 1 table spoon / 5g. (recommended)........... *
Coix (seeds) YiYi Ren 1 table spoon / 5g. (recommended) .... *
Rice wild (nature rice) 1 1/2 cups / 240g. (yes) .... metal
Water 8-10 cups / 800g. (yes) .... earth

Cooking instructions:
Each one 1 tbsp: Bai He, Longan, Yu Zhu, Da Zao, Shan Yao, Lian Mi, Yi Yi Ren, Qian Shi
Add hot water and soak for about 30 minutes. Then add 1 - 2 cups of rice (normal) and simmer for 1/2 to 1 hour until the rice is very soft. Or: Cook for about 3 hours with the herbs a congee. Then the herbs do not have to be soaked.

9.2 Basic recipe for a beef broth (clear)

Strengthens Qi and Yang, is very warming.
Cooking time approx. 4-8 hours
Calories p. portion: 114
10 portions
Allergens: O

Quantity of ingredients

Beef soup meat 1,1 lbs / 500g. .... earth
Beef meatbones 5/8 oz / 200g. .... earth
Vinegar (Red wine vinegar) 1 dash / 3g. .... wood
Juniper berry 8 pieces / 6g. .... fire
Rosemary 1 pinch / 1g. .... fire
Carrot 3 pieces / 210g. .... earth
Parsnip 2 pieces / 300g. .... fire
Leek 1 piece / 200g. .... metal
Ginger fresh 1/2 teaspoon / 5g. .... metal
Lovage 1 stem / 15g. .... metal
Clove 2 pieces / 2g. .... metal
Pimento 6 pieces / 12g. .... metal
Anise (Common Fennel) 2 pieces / 1g. .... earth
Salt 1 teaspoon / 5g. .... water
Water 3,3 lbs / 1300g. .... earth

Cooking instructions:
Heat water, a dash of red wine vinegar, some juniper berries, a little rosemary, bones and meat till it boils; add carrot, parsnip, leek, ginger, lovage, clove, allspice, star anise and a little salt; simmer for 4-8 hours then strain.
Refrigerate for later use.

9.3   Basic recipe for a chicken broth worming

Strengthens Qi and blood, is very warm.
Cooking time approx. 2-3 hours
Calories p. portion: 90
9 portions
Allergens: L

Quantity of ingredients

Chicken meat 1/2 piece / 600g. .... wood
Carrot 2 pieces / 150g. .... earth
Leek 1 stick / 45g. .... metal
Celery root 1 piece / 500g. .... earth
Ginger fresh 2 slices / 2g. .... metal
Fenugreek (Trigonella foenum-graecum) 1 teaspoon / 2g. .... *
Juniper berry 1 teaspoon / 3g. .... fire
Bay leaf 3 pieces / 2g. .... *
Water 4 cup / 900g. .... earth

Cooking instructions:
Remove chicken parts from fat. Place chicken pieces in a saucepan with hot water and heat till it boils briefly, skimming any resulting foam. Add coarsely chopped vegetables and all spices and cook over medium heat for 2 to 3 hours. Strain the finished soup. Throw away vegetables and bones.
Tip: If you want to use the meat as a soup insert, take out after 45 minutes and return only the bones in the soup.
Refrigerate for later use.

9.4   Basic recipe for a duck broth

Forces Qi, strengthens blood and fluids, nourishes Yin, forces stomach, cools heat, strengthens spleen and liver.
Cooking time approx. 2-3 hours
Calories p. portion: 61
6 portions
Allergens: L

Quantity of ingredients
Duck (heart) 5/8 oz / 200g. ....wood
Water 2 cup / 450g. .... earth
Duck (slaughtered) 1/4 lbs - 4oz / 100g. ....wood
Carrot 2 pieces / 100g. .... earth
Celery root 1/2 piece / 600g. .... earth

Cooking instructions:
Cook duck pieces with vegetables for 2-3 hours. Sift broth through a fine sieve and refrigerate for later use.

The innards can be reused: You cut them finely and leaves them for a few minutes with fresh vegetables in the broth draw. Sprinkle with parsley before serving.

9.5   Basic recipe for a fish broth

Strengthens kidney Qi and Yin, strengthens blood and fluids, promotes urination.
Cooking time approx. 40 min
Calories p. portion: 128
5 portions
Allergens: DLO

Quantity of ingredients

Fish pieces mixed (fresh water) 3/4 lbs / 300g. ....water
Celery root 1/4 lbs - 4oz / 120g. .... earth
Leek 2 inches / 10g. ....metal
Carrot 2 pieces / 150g. .... earth
White wine 1/2 cup / 125g. ....wood
Lemon 1/2 piece / 50g. ....wood
Bay leaf 2 leaves / 2g. ....*
Peppercorns 3 pieces / 2g. ....metal
Olive oil 1 table spoon / 10g. .... earth
Water 2 cup / 450g. .... earth

Cooking instructions:

Fry celery, chopped carrots and leeks in olive oil, add bay leaf and
peppercorns, add pieces of fish and sauté briefly. Add water, add little
white wine or lemon. Simmer gently for 30 minutes. Skim off the
resulting foam several times. In the end, sift the ingredients through a
cloth.
Refrigerate for later use.

9.6 Basic recipe for a reissue soup (Congee)

Warms the stomach and spleen, harmonizes the intestine, forces Qi,
reduces moisture.
Cooking time approx. 2-4 hours
Calories p. portion: 140
3 portions
Allergens:

Quantity of ingredients

Rice variety any 1 cup / 120g. ....metal
Water 6 cups / 700g. .... earth

Cooking instructions:

Cook rice and water in a ratio of about 1: 6. The amount of water
determines the thickness of the mash (matter of taste).
Put the rice in a saucepan with a heavy lid. It is important to simmer the
rice after a short boil on the slightest flame, otherwise it burns.
Boil the rice for 2-4 hours. The longer he cooks, the more he
strengthens.
If you want to eat the dish for breakfast, you can put the rice on just
before bedtime.
To be on the safe side, you should first check the behavior of your pot

and cooker under observation for a similar amount of time, so that nothing burns.
Refrigerate for later use.

9.7   Basic recipe for a vegetable soup, nutritious

Strengthens spleen and lung, regulates Qi flow, builds up Qi, dries out, passes downwardly, strengthens stomach Qi.
Cooking time approx. 2-3 hours
Calories p. portion: 48
5 portions
Allergens: L

Quantity of ingredients
Olive oil 1 table spoon / 4g. .... earth
Onion white 1 piece / 60g. ....metal
Carrot 3 pieces / 200g. .... earth
Parsnip 3/8 lbs - 6oz / 150g. .... fire
Celery root 1 cup / 100g. .... earth
Ginger fresh 1/2 teaspoon / 2g. ....metal
Lemon 1/2 piece / 25g. .... wood
Juniper berry 6 pieces / 6g. .... fire
Thyme dried 1 pinch / 1g. ....metal
Lovage 1 table spoon / 3g. ....metal
Bay leaf 2 leaves / 1g. .... *
Salt 1 pinch / 1g. .... water
Water 3 cups / 650g. .... earth

Cooking instructions:
Cut the vegetables into cubes.
Heat oil in hot pot, fry shortly onions and vegetables.
Add cold water, then add ginger, bay leaf and lemon juice.
Season with juniper, thyme and lovage. Cover for 2 - 3 hours on a low heat and simmer.
The used vegetables should be thrown away.
The basic recipe serves as a soup base and to refine vegetables, legumes or cereals.
If you want to eat vegetable soup immediately, add the desired vegetables half an hour before.
Refrigerate for later use.

9.8 Beef broth

Warming and nourishing, builds up Qi, strengthens blood and fluids.
Cooking time approx. 2-6 hours
Calories p. portion: 125
7 portions
Allergens: L

Quantity of ingredients
Water 4 cup / 1000g. (yes) .... earth
Lemon 2 dashes / 2g. .... wood
Beef meat 1,1 lbs / 500g. (yes) .... earth
Beef meatbones 2 pieces / 0g. (yes) .... earth
Turmeric (yellow root) 1 pinch / 1g. (recommended) .... *
Carrot 2 pieces / 100g. (recommended) .... earth
Celery root 1 inch / 25g. (recommended) .... earth
Parsley root 1 piece / 150g. (recommended) .... earth
Onion white 1 piece / 50g. (yes) .... metal
Bay leaf 2-3 leaves / 2g. (recommended) .... *
Coriander 1/2 teaspoon / 2g. (yes) .... metal
Ginger fresh 1 inch / 2g. (recommended) .... metal
Wakame 1 inch / 1g. (recommended) .... water
Parsley 1 stem / 10g. (yes) .... wood

Cooking instructions:
In a saucepan with water (enough to cover the meat), add a few drops
of lemon juice, a little turmeric, beef and bones, heat till it boils and
simmer for a while; then pour away the whole broth, clean the pot, rinse
off meat and bones with hot water (this will save you from foaming) and
put it back to the saucepan with hot water (amount as you like); add a
good pinch of turmeric, carrot, celery, parsley root to the pot; add onion,
bay leaves, coriander, a piece of sliced ginger, a strip of wakame, a
stalk of parsley; boil everything together and simmer for 2-6 hours (if the
meat is to be used otherwise, take it out of the broth after 1 1/2 - 2
hours, as soon as it is cooked, the bones are returned to the broth);
When the cooking time is over, pour the broth through a sieve and
discard all ingredients.

Notes: The longer the broth has cooked, the warmer but more
nourishing it is. It is after cooling for 3-4 days in the refrigerator durable.
The broth can be drunk hot or used as a base for soups with cereals,
potatoes and fresh vegetables.

9.9 Beef soup with carrots, leeks, bay leaves

Strengthens spleen Qi, strengthens blood and Qi, moisturizes, relaxes, builds up Qi, spreads, strengthens spleen and liver, regulates Qi flow, strengthens stomach Qi.
Cooking time approx. 2-3 hours
Calories p. portion: 194
5 portions

Quantity of ingredients
Beef meat 1 lbs / 500g. (yes)... earth
Carrot 2 pieces / 200g. (recommended).................................... earth
Leek 1/2 piece / 150g. (recommended) ....metal
Bay leaf 3 leaves / 1g. (recommended) .... *
Corn Grease (Polenta) 1 table spoon / 10g. (yes)...................... earth
Water 2 cup / 450g. (yes)... earth
Salt 1 pinch / 0,5g. (recommended)...water

Cooking instructions:
In a saucepan with water (enough to cover the meat), add beef soup meat or leg slice and simmer for a moment; then pour off the broth, rinse the meat with hot water (this will save you from foaming), clean the pot and put the meat in hot water again; add chopped carrot, leek, corn and bay leaf; simmer until the meat is cooked.

9.10 Beluga lentil stew with vegetables

Tonifies Qi and blood, forces kidneys and spleen, dissipates heat and moisture.
Cooking time approx. 20 min
Calories p. portion: 201
5 portions

Quantity of ingredients
Lentils 1 1/2 cups / 240g. (yes)..water
Water 4-5 cups / 500g. (yes) .... earth
Carrot 3 pieces / 150g. (recommended).................................... earth
Leek 1 piece / 300g. (recommended) ....metal
Kohlrabi 1/2 piece / 200g. (recommended) .... earth
Tomato 2 pieces / 80g. .... wood
Onion white 1 piece / 50g. (yes) ....metal
Bay leaf 2 leaves / 1g. (recommended) .... *

Fennel 1 piece / 250g. (yes)... earth
Star anise 2 pieces / 1g. (yes) .... *
Juniper berry 6 pieces / 2g. (recommended)............................... fire
Olive oil 2 table spoons / 30g. (yes)... earth
Salt 1 pinch / 1g. (recommended)...water
Ginger fresh 1/2 teaspoon / 2g. (recommended).......................metal
Black caraway 1 pinch / 1g. (recommended) .... *

Cooking instructions:
Heat oil in hot pot. Fry onions and add diced vegetables and spices, lentils (washed well) and salt. Cover with cold water (3 fingers wide) and cook for 20 minutes on a low heat.
Sprinkle with fresh herbs and black cumin

Goes well with rice!

9.11 Black-eyed beans stew

Strengthens spleen and kidney, is very nutritious, warms the stomach and spleen, harmonizes the intestine, forces Qi, strengthens stomach and kidney, strengthens spleen and kidney.
Cooking time approx. 20 min
Calories p. portion: 140
5 portions

Quantity of ingredients
Black-eyed peas 1 cup / 100g. (yes)...water
Rice variety any 1 1/2 cups / 200g. (yes) ....metal
Water 10 cups / 1000g. (yes).. earth

Cooking instructions:
Soak the beans overnight and strain.

In a ratio of 1: 2, simmer the beans together with the rice in the Water. Depending on how hot the flame is and how thin the dish should be, more water must be added.

Variation: Add vegetables fried in oil, such as carrots, celery tubers, onions or leeks.

9.12 Boiled fillet with potatoebiscuits (Austrian Tafelspitz)

Strengthens spleen Qi, strengthens blood and Qi, moisturizes, relaxes, builds up Qi, spreads, forces Qi, forces spleen, relieves inflammation, moisturizes.
Cooking time approx. 3 hours
Calories p. portion: 454
8 portions
Allergens: L

Quantity of ingredients
Onion white 1 piece / 50g. (yes) .... metal
Corn germ oil 1 table spoon / 10g. (recommended) .... earth
Water 32 cup - 1 gallon / 0g. (yes) .... earth
Beef meat 5,4 lbs - 70oz cap of rump / 1800g. (yes) .... earth
Beef meatbones 4n slices with bone marrow / 0g. (yes) .... earth
Salt 1 pinch / 0,5g. (recommended) .... water
Peppercorns 15 pieces / 0g. (little) .... metal
Parsnip 1 piece / 0g. (recommended) .... fire
Carrot 2 pieces / 0g. (recommended) .... earth
Celery root 1 slice / 0g. (recommended) .... earth
Parsley root 2 pieces / 0g. (recommended) .... earth
Leek 1/2 stick / 0g. (recommended) .... metal
Chives 1 table spoon (chopped) / 7g. (yes) .... metal
Potato 2,2 lbs / 1000g. (yes) .... earth
Sunflower oil 2 table spoons / 20g. (yes) .... earth
Salt 1 pinch / 0,5g. (recommended) .... water

Cooking instructions:
Halve the onions, but do not peel. Brown onions in a pan with fat on the cut surfaces very dark. Wash meat and bones briefly with warm water, drain.
Heat the water till it boils, put in meat and cook gently. Always scoop up rising foam. As soon as no more foam rises, add peppercorns and the onion. Clean and cut root and leeks and add after about two and a half hours cooking time. Simmer for another half hour.
Remove boiled beef from the soup, pour through a sieve and season with salt. Cut roots into bite-sized pieces. Add the soup together with the marrow bones and leave it under the boiling point. Cut the boiled beef into finger-
thick slices against the grain, place in the soup, heat again, sprinkle with a little chives. In addition, cook and peel the potatoes in salted

water. Stomp roughly or cut finely. Fry in a pan with the oil crispy.

9.13 Carp soup

Nourishing and slightly warming, strengthens the middle and the lower heater, removes moisture.
Cooking time approx. 2 hours
Calories p. portion: 499
2 portions
Allergens: DO

Quantity of ingredients
Carp 1,1 lbs / 500g. (yes)..water
Salt 1 pinch / 1g. (recommended)..water
Vinegar (Apple vinegar) 1 teaspoon / 3g. (yes)........................wood
Thyme 1 Twig / 3g. (yes)...*
Juniper berry 8 pieces / 3g. (recommended)............................... fire
Carrot 2 pieces / 200g. (recommended)................................... earth
Leek 1 piece / 200g. (recommended) ....metal
Onion white 1 piece / 60g. (yes) ....metal
Ginger fresh 1/2 teaspoon / 2g. (recommended)......................metal
Bay leaf 3 leaves / 1g. (recommended) ....*
White wine 1/2 cup / 125g. (recommended)..............................wood
Basil 3 leaves / 1g. (yes) ....metal

Cooking instructions:
Preparation: When shopping at the fishmonger, remove the fillets from a medium-sized, whole carp and also pack the fish head, spine with bones and tail.

Cut the fillets into 1 cm cubes; salt and set aside.

Place fish head, backbone and tail of carp in plenty of cold water; heat till it boils and scoop the foam; add a dash of vinegar, a fresh sprig of thyme, juniper berries; Add carrot, a piece of leek and chopped onion; add a thick slice of ginger, some peppercorns, 1 bay leaf, salt; simmer for about 1 1/2 hours and pour the stock through a sieve.
Put the carp pieces in a saucepan; pour a shot of white wine; Add rose paprika, basil leaves, finely ground carrots, dried thyme and the stock and warm; Boil the ingredients for about 5 minutes until the fish pieces are cooked.
Variants: Thicken the soup with kudzu or mashed potatoes.
This fits: baguette and dry white wine.

9.14 Chicken soup with angelica root and buckthorn fruit

Strengthens spleen and nourishes the blood and Yin of the liver, forces Qi and blood, is very warming.
Cooking time approx. 1 1/2 hours
Calories p. portion: 77
3 portions
Allergens: LO

Quantity of ingredients
Basic recipe for a chicken soup 2 cup / 500g. (recommended)..........*
Angelica root 1/8 oz / 5g. (recommended) ....*
Bocksdorn fruits, goji berry dried 1/8 lbs - 2oz / 50g. (yes) ....wood

Cooking instructions:
When you cook chicken broth according to basic recipes add angelica root and Bocksdorn fruits in the last 40 minutes.
Ingestion: Drink 2-3 cups of broth daily.

9.15 Clear oxen tail soup with buckthorn fruit

Forces Qi, nourishes the liver blood, good for ocular fibrillation or dry eyes, muscle tension or calf cramps due to blood deficiency.
Cooking time approx. 1-2 hours
Calories p. portion: 217
6 portions
Allergens: O

Quantity of ingredients
Basic recipe for a beef soup 4 cup / 1000g. (recommended).............*
Beef Oxtail pieces 1,1 lbs / 500g. (recommended).....................earth
Shiitake, dried 4-5 pieces / 4g. (recommended)........................earth
Onion white 1 piece / 60g. (yes) ....metal
Sake 2 table spoons / 20g. (recommended)..............................metal
Ginger fresh 1/2 teaspoon / 2g. (recommended).......................metal
Bocksdorn fruits, goji berry dried 1 table spoon / 8g. (yes) ....wood

Cooking instructions:
Soak shiitake mushrooms. Blanch oxtail slices (This removes fat and impurities). Cook in the beef broth for 1-2 hours.
Then add the spring onions, shiitake mushrooms, rice wine, buckthorn fruits and ginger and simmer gently.

9.16 Clear soup from goose

Forces spleen, stomach and lungs, relieves weakness, forces Qi, calms the stomach, gets Qi moving, directs upwards, strengthens spleen and liver, regulates Qi flow, moisturizes, relaxes, builds up Qi, spreads.
Cooking time approx. 2-3 hours
Calories p. portion: 334
6 portions

Quantity of ingredients
Goose parts 1,1 lbs / 500g. (yes)..metal
Carrot 1 piece / 100g. (recommended) .... earth
Onion (shallot) 1 piece / 25g. (yes)..metal
Leek 1 piece / 250g. (recommended) ....metal
Parsley 1 Twig / 4g. (yes)..wood
Lovage 1 Twig / 4g. (yes)..metal
Chervil 1 pinch / 0,2g. (recommended)...*
Water 4 cup / 1000g. (yes) .... earth
Salt 1 pinch / 0,5g. (recommended)..water

Cooking instructions:
Simmer goose pieces with vegetables and herbs for 2-3 hours. Sift through a fine cloth and cool. Degrease and store in the refrigerator.

9.17 Coconut rice with cardamom

Forces lungs and spleen, diuretic, forces Qi, protects liver, forces stomach and spleen, forces muscles, reduces moisture, strengthens Qi and Kidney Jing, strengthens Qi of the heart and lungs, quenches thirst.
Cooking time approx. 45 min
Calories p. portion: 266
4 portions
Allergens: GO

Quantity of ingredients
Rice long grain rice 1 cup / 120g. (yes).....................................metal
Water 6 cups / 400g. (yes) .... earth
Sugar cane sugar 1 table spoon / 10g. .... earth
Cardamom 1 teaspoon / 2g. (recommended)...................................*
Ginger fresh 1/2 teaspoon / 2g. (recommended)......................metal
Butter organic 2 table spoons / 20g. (yes)............................... earth
Coconut grated 2 table spoons / 16g. (yes) .... earth
Cashews 1 table spoon / 8g. (yes).. earth
Raisins 1 table spoon / 8g. (recommended).............................. earth

Salt 1 pinch / 0,5g. (recommended)..water
Lemon 1/2 piece / 15g. ....wood
Pumpkin 3/4 lbs / 300g. (yes).. earth
Olive oil 2 table spoons / 20g. (yes).. earth
Coriander 1 pinch / 0,2g. (yes) ....metal
Pepper (ground) 1 pinch / 0,2g. (little)....................................metal
Curry 1 pinch / 0,5g. ....metal
Water 1/4 cup / 50g. (yes).. earth
Salt 1 pinch / 0,5g. (recommended)..water
Parsley 1 table spoon / 8g. (yes) ....wood
Cardamom 1 pinch / 0,2g. (recommended)......................................*
Turmeric (yellow root) 1 pinch / 0,2g. (recommended) ....*

Cooking instructions:
Preparation: Soak long grain rice in cold water for 1 hour and drain.

Then: Heat fresh water till it boils; add some whole cane sugar, plenty of ground cardamom or some cardamom pods, grated ginger and the rice into the hot water and cook.

Separately: heat some butter in a hot pot; add grated coconut, cashews and raisins; add the cooked rice and salt; pour lemon juice over it; mix everything and let it pass for a few minutes.

Pumpkin vegetables: heat olive oil in a pan. Steam the pumpkin (cut in cubes), season with cilantro, pepper and curry, simmer with a little water, salt with sea salt, add chopped parsley with cardamom and turmeric, simmer on a small fire for about 10 minutes, depending on the pumpkin, the pumpkin should still be firm.

9.18 Cod soup with tomatoes

Strengthens kidney Qi, strengthens blood and fluids, promotes urination, forces Qi from spleen and kidney, softens, passes downwardly, scatters and move Qi, moisturizes, reduces cold-evil, softens knots, nourishes liver-Yin.
Cooking time approx. 30 min
Calories p. portion: 176
4 portions
Allergens: DLO

Quantity of ingredients

Basic recipe for a fish soup 2 cup / 450g. (recommended)............... *
Cod 5/8 lbs - 8oz / 250g. (yes)...water
Onion (shallot) 1 piece / 20g. (yes)..metal
Anise (Common Fennel) 1/2 teaspoon / 1g. (yes)...................... earth
Ginger fresh 1/2 teaspoon / 1g. (recommended)........................metal
Olive oil 1 teaspoon / 3g. (yes) .... earth
Tomato 1 piece / 50g. ....wood
White wine 1/2 cup / 125g. (recommended).............................wood
Salt 1 pinch / 0,5g. (recommended)..water
Pepper (ground) 1 pinch / 0,2g. (little)......................................metal
Parsley 1 table spoon (chopped) / 5g. (yes).............................wood

Cooking instructions:
Fry the onion, anise and freshly grated ginger in oil.
Add finely chopped tomatoes and sauté. Add a little wine and fish soup.
Simmer gently for 10-15 minutes. Season with salt and pepper; Add the
cod pieces and heat gently. Garnish with parsley at the end.

9.19 Fish soup with white wine, laurel and marjoram

Strengthens kidney Qi, strengthens blood and fluids, promotes
urination, moisturizes, softens knots, regulates Qi, dries out, passes
downwardly, relaxes, builds up Qi.
Cooking time approx. 45 min
Calories p. portion: 200
3 portions
Allergens: DLO

Quantity of ingredients

Onion (spring onion) 2 pieces / 40g. (yes) ....metal
Garlic 1 clove / 2g. (recommended)..metal
Basic recipe for a fish soup 2 cup / 500g. (recommended)............... *
Carrot 1 piece / 60g. (recommended) .... earth
Parsnip 1 piece / 100g. (recommended) .... fire
Celery root 1 slice / 60g. (recommended) .... earth
Salt 1 pinch / 1g. (recommended)..water
Peppercorns 2 pieces / 1g. (little) ....metal
Lemon 1/4 piece / 10g. ....wood
White wine 1/2 cup / 125g. (recommended).............................wood
Bay leaf 2 leaves / 1g. (recommended) .... *

Rosemary 1 teaspoon / 2g. (recommended)................................. fire
Chives 1 teaspoon (chopped) / 3g. (yes) ....metal
Parsley 1 teaspoon (chopped) / 3g. (yes) ....wood

Cooking instructions:
Fry the onion and garlic in oil until translucent. Add fish broth. Add the diced carrot, parsnip and celery. Season with salt and peppercorns. Simmer the soup on a low heat for 25 minutes.
Wash the fish, drizzle with lemon juice, divide into pieces and add to the soup with the wine, the bay leaves and the marjoram. Cook for 5 min on low heat.
Add the chives and parsley and season the soup with the salt.

9.20 Hummus (Chickpeasmash)

Strengthens spleen and heart, softens, passes downwardly, moisturizes, relaxes, builds up Qi, spreads, nourishes blood, nourishes blood and liver, harmonizes liver and spleen, forces eyesight, preserves the fluids, contracts.
Cooking time approx. 2 hours
Calories p. portion: 542
2 portions
Allergens: N

Quantity of ingredients
Chickpeas 1 1/2 cups / 240g. (recommended)...........................water
Wakame 1 teaspoon (grated) / 2g. (recommended)...................water
Ginger fresh 1/4 teaspoon / 1g. (recommended).......................metal
Rosemary 1 pinch / 0,5g. (recommended).................................... fire
Sesame paste (Tahini) 1 table spoon / 10g. (recommended) ..... earth
Olive oil 2 table spoons / 20g. (yes)... earth
Lemon juice 1 dash / 2g. ....wood
Water upon need / g. (yes).. earth
Garlic 1 clove (scraped) / 2g. (recommended) ....metal
Parsley 1 teaspoon (chopped) / 2g. (yes) ....wood
Peppers 1 pinch / 0,2g. (yes)... earth
Curcuma 1 pinch / 0,2g. (recommended)...*
Coriander 1 pinch / 0,2g. (yes) ....metal
Cardamom 1 pinch / 0,2g. (recommended)...*
Pepper (ground) 1 pinch / 0,2g. (little)....................................metal
Salt (herbal) 1/2 teaspoon / 2g. (recommended).......................water

Cooking instructions:
Soak chickpeas overnight or for at least 6 hours, pour off soaking water, boil in fresh water for about 1 to 1 ½ hours with a little seaweed and ginger, allow to cool.
Seasoning with a few splashes of lemon juice and parsley.
Add the pepper, garlic cut into small pieces or pressed, more or less coriander and cardamom powder, little chili powder as desired, tahin and olive oil.

Puree all ingredients together. Depending on the consistency, add water. It should be a smooth paste.
Spread on cereal, crackers or toasted bread or enjoy with salad.

9.21 Japanese algae soup

Strengthens spleen and liver, regulates Qi flow, moisturizes, relaxes, builds up Qi, spreads, nourishes the lungs and spleen, distributes mucus, dissolves mucus, dissolves stagnation, directs upwards, gets Qi moving und Yang.
Cooking time approx. 20 min
Calories p. portion: 47
3 portions

Quantity of ingredients
Wakame 1 oz / 25g. (recommended)...water
Water 2 cup / 450g. (yes)... earth
Onion (shallot) 1-2 pcs. / 30g. (yes).............................metal
Radish (white, green, purple-red) 1/8 lbs - 2oz / 50g. (yes)........metal
Carrot 2 pieces / 180g. (recommended)................................... earth
Miso 2 table spoons / 20g. (yes)...............................water
Parsley 2 table spoons / 20g. (yes)............................... wood
Onion (spring onion) 1 table spoon (sliced)..............................metal

Cooking instructions:
Soak wakame in water for a few minutes, remove and bring the water to the boil. Add finely chopped onions and wakame, radishes and carrots, cut into thin strips, and simmer for another 10 minutes. Dissolve miso in a little cooled cooking water and add it at the end. Sprinkle with parsley and spring onions.

9.22 Legumes

Strengthens spleen and liver, regulates Qi flow, moisturizes, relaxes, builds up Qi, spreads, nourishes blood and Qi, diuretic, harmonizes Qi (in the middle and lower heater), detoxifies, reduces internal heat and moisture.
Cooking time approx. 30 min
Calories p. portion: 31
5 portions

Quantity of ingredients
Pinto beans speckled 1/4 lbs - 4oz / 100g. (recommended) ....water
Lentils 1/8 lbs - 2oz / 50g. (yes)..water
Peas, green 1/8 lbs - 2oz / 50g. (yes) ....water
Water 4 cup / 1000g. (yes) .... earth
Lemon 1 slice / 2g. ....wood
Juniper berry 6 pieces / 2g. (recommended)............................... fire
Thyme 1 Twig / 3g. (yes)..*
Rosemary 1 Twig / 3g. (recommended)....................................... fire
Carrot 1 piece / 100g. (recommended) .... earth
Savory 1-2 teaspoons / 5g. (yes)...water
Ginger fresh a great piece / 3g. (recommended).........................metal
Bay leaf 2-3 leaves / 1g. (recommended) ....*
Wakame 1-2 strips / 1g. (recommended)....................................water

Cooking instructions:
Legumes such as beans, lentils, peas or chickpeas are soaked in plenty of cold water for several hours to three days. The water should be changed every 8 hours. Then pour off soaking water and wash legumes thoroughly.

Preparation:
Cook the legumes with fresh cold water and a slice of ginger and bring to froth. Cook without lid for about 5 minutes, scooping off the foam. Only then add the following ingredients: a slice of lemon or lemon juice, crush juniper berries, thyme; (possibly 1 knife tip of asafoetida in case of severe indigestion). Add savory, sage, juniper, fenugreek seeds, carrots, bay leaves, fresh ginger, wakame algae.

Simmer on the slightest flame until beans or lentils have the desired consistency.
This base can be stored for 3-4 days in the refrigerator.

9.23 Lentils and rice stew

Strengthens spleen and liver, regulates Qi flow, moisturizes, relaxes, builds up Qi, spreads, warms the stomach and spleen, harmonizes the intestine, forces Qi, reduces moisture, brings the liver Qi in motion, cools heat.
Cooking time approx. 25 min
Calories p. portion: 232
3 portions
Allergens: LNO

Quantity of ingredients
Lentils 1/4 lbs - 4oz / 100g. (yes)..water
Water 5 cups / 500g. (yes) .... earth
Rice variety any 1 cup / 120g. (yes)..metal
Sesame oil 1 table spoon / 10g. (yes)..................................... earth
Carrot 2 pieces / 150g. (recommended)................................... earth
Celery sticks 2 rods / 20g. (yes) .... earth
Cumin (Caraway seed) 1 pinch / 0,2g. (yes) ....metal
Salt 1 pinch / 0,5g. (recommended)...water
Vinegar (Apple vinegar) 1 dash / 2g. (yes)................................ wood
Parsley 2 table spoons / 18g. (yes)..wood

Cooking instructions:
Soak the dry lentils the day before.
Heat sesame oil in a hot pot; cut carrot and celery into small pieces and sauté; add rice, a pinch of cumin and lentils and heat till it boils.
If the lenses are soft, add salt; season with a little vinegar and garnish with parsley.

Variant: In summer you can omit the cumin and add fresh green peas, Chinese cabbage or celery.

9.24 Millet with egg and butter

Forces blood, Yin and Jing, nourishes Yin, moisturizes in case of internal dryness, forces blood, forces spleen, calms nerves and stomach, strengthens spleen and kidney, diuretic, strengthens Qi and kidney Jing, moisturizes, relaxes, builds up Qi, spreads.
Cooking time approx. 25 min
Calories p. portion: 338
2 portions
Allergens: CG

Quantity of ingredients
Millet 1 cup / 100g. (yes) .... earth
Ginger fresh 1/2 teaspoon / 1g. (recommended) .... metal
Salt 1 pinch / 0,5g. (recommended) .... water
Parsley 2 table spoons / 16g. (yes) .... wood
Pepper powder (hot) 1 pinch / 1g. (recommended) .... fire
Chicken egg 2 pieces / 100g. (recommended) .... earth
Butter organic 2 table spoons / 20g. (yes) .... earth
Nutmeg 1 pinch / 0,2g. (recommended) .... metal
Water 1 1/2 cups / 200g. (yes) .... earth

Cooking instructions:
Simmer the millet with the ginger and nutmeg in the water for 5 min.
and let it swell for another 30 min.
Cook and peel 1 soft egg per person; pile up the millet on plates and
place 1 egg each in a hollow in the millet mountain; Put butterflakes
over it. Sprinkle with chopped parsley and the rose paprika.

9.25 Mung bean stew

Dissipates excess heat, is very nutritious, reduces heat and poison,
softens, passes downwardly, warms the stomach and spleen,
harmonizes the intestine, forces Qi, reduces moisture.
Cooking time approx. 2 hours
Calories p. portion: 665
2 portions

Quantity of ingredients
Mung bean 5/8 lbs - 8oz - 500g / 300g. (yes) .... water
Sunflower oil 2 table spoons / 30g. (yes) .... earth
Amaranth 1/2 teaspoon / 2g. (recommended) .... fire
Fennel seeds ground 1/2 teaspoon / 2g. (recommended) .... earth
Cumin (Caraway seed) 1/2 teaspoon / 2g. (yes) .... metal
Coriander 1/2 teaspoon / 2g. (yes) .... metal
Rice round grain 1/2 cup / 60g. (yes) .... metal
Water 3 cups / 300g. (yes) .... earth
Ginger fresh 1 inch / 3g. (recommended) .... metal
Kombu seaweed 1 inch / 2g. (recommended) .... water
Salt 1 pinch / 0,5g. (recommended) .... water
Parsley 1 table spoon / 3g. (yes) .... wood

Cooking instructions:
Soak mung beans overnight.
Heat sunflower oil in a hot pot. Stir in the amaranth, fennel seeds, cumin and coriander and fry briefly.
admit basmati rice, some ginger and mung beans and roast briefly.
Pour water and heat till it boils.
Add a piece of kombu alga and salt.
Simmer for 1-1/2 hours.
Garnish with parsley or coriander.

9.26 Pea dish

Strengthens the middle, diuretic, harmonizes Qi (in the middle and lower heater), detoxifies, softens, passes downwardly, forces blood, Yin and Jing, nourishes Yin, moisturizes in case of internal dryness.
Cooking time approx. 1-2 hours
Calories p. portion: 406
1 portions
Allergens: CE

Quantity of ingredients
Peas 3/8 lbs - 6oz (dried) / 150g. (yes) .... water
Lemon 1 piece / 40g. .... wood
Juniper berry 6 pieces / 2g. (recommended) .... fire
Sunflower oil 1 teaspoon / 3g. (yes) .... earth
Pepper white (ground) 1 pinch / 0,3g. (little) .... metal
Bay leaf 3 leaves / 2g. (recommended) .... *
Onion white 1 piece / 50g. (yes) .... metal
Thyme 1 teaspoon / 2g. (yes) .... *
Ginger fresh 1/2 teaspoon / 1g. (recommended) .... metal
Chicken egg 1 piece / 60g. (recommended) .... earth
Wakame 1 inch / 2g. (recommended) .... water
Salt 1 pinch / 1g. (recommended) .... water
Soy sauce per taste / 2g. .... water

Cooking instructions:
Soak dried peas in plenty of cold water for several hours or overnight.
Pour away soaking water and wash peas thoroughly.

Place the peas with about 1 1/2 l of cold water and heat till it boils; cook without lid for 5 minutes; scoop up the foam that forms; only then add the following ingredients: a slice of lemon, juniper berries, oil, peppercorns, bay leaves, chopped onion, dried thyme, chopped ginger, simmer about 2 strips of wakame or 1 tbsp Hijiki with lid closed for 1 - 2 hours; After 1 hour, try if the peas are already soft, because the cooking time changes with the soaking time and the age of aging; when the peas are cooked, remove the lemon slice, juniper berries and peppercorns; with salt, soy sauce, lemon juice to taste.

Note: The dish can be refrigerated for 3-4 days and heated in portions.

Serve with: crispy vegetables, rice or millet steamed in water.

9.27 Polenta with fried egg

Nourishing and slightly warming, builds up Qi, forces blood, Yin and Jing, strengthens stomach Qi, diuretic, moisturizes, relaxes, builds up Qi, spreads, gets Qi moving, forces fluids production, reduces cold-evil. Not: in wet heat of the gallbladder.
Cooking time approx. 15 min
Calories p. portion: 410
2 portions
Allergens: CG

Quantity of ingredients
Water 1 1/2 cups / 200g. (yes)... earth
Corn Grease (Polenta) 1 cup / 120g. (yes) .... earth
Ginger fresh 1 pinch / 0,5g. (recommended)............................metal
Butter organic 1/2 teaspoon / 2g. (yes)..................................... earth
Pepper (ground) 1 pinch / 0,2g. (little)....................................metal
Nutmeg 1 pinch / 0,2g. (recommended)...................................metal
Salt 1 pinch / 0,5g. (recommended)..water
Lemon juice 1 dash / 1g. ....wood
Pepper powder (hot) 1 pinch / 0,3g. (recommended) .... fire
Chicken egg 4 pieces / 250g. (recommended)...........................earth
Chives 2 table spoons / 14g. (yes)...metal

Cooking instructions:
Stir in a saucepan with hot water polenta and a little ginger; swell until the polenta is cooked.
Add a piece of butter, pepper, nutmeg, salt, a few drops of lemon, a pinch of rose paprika.
Put the polenta in a fireproof bowl.
Put 1 fried egg per person on top; bake in the oven for a few minutes, so that the egg yolk is still liquid.
Sprinkle with ground pepper, finely chopped chives and a little salt.

9.28 Porridge with raisins and sake

Forces Qi, nourishes fluids, moisturises dryness, produces humors, moisturizes intestines, cools inner heat, scatters and move Qi, moisturizes, reduces cold-evil, softens knots.
Cooking time approx. 10 min
Calories p. portion: 427
1 portions
Allergens: AGO

Quantity of ingredients
Oat flakes (whole grain) 8 table spoons / 60g. (yes)...................metal
Water 1/2 cup / 125g. (yes)...................... earth
Cow's milk (whole milk 3.5% fat) 1/2 cup / 125g. (little).....................*
Salt 1 pinch / 1g. (recommended).................................water
Cream, sweet 30% 2 table spoons / 20g. (recommended)...............*
Raisins 1 table spoon / 15g. (recommended)............................ earth
Sake 1 table spoon / 10g. (recommended) ....metal

Cooking instructions:
Heat water and milk and a pinch of salt till it boils. Sprinkle in 4 tablespoons of coarse rolled oats and cook to a pulp, add 4 tablespoons of fine oatmeal, allow to simmer. Arrange in a preheated bowl and top with cream.
Add raisins and sake.

9.29 Quinoa piquant with avocado

Nourishes Yin from liver, lungs and colon, moisturizes, relaxes, builds up Qi, spreads, strengthens spleen and liver, regulates Qi flow, moisturizes, relaxes, builds up Qi, spreads, forces Qi, dries out, regulates Qi, warms spleen and kidney, dissolves stagnation
Cooking time approx. 20 min
Calories p. portion: 561
2 portions

Quantity of ingredients
Water 1 1/2 cups / 240g. (yes)..................... earth
Quinoa 1 cup / 100g. (recommended) .... fire
Carrot 1 piece shredded / 100g. (recommended)...................... earth
Onion (spring onion) 2 table spoons (chopped) / 12g. (yes).......metal
Curcuma 1/2 teaspoon / 1g. (recommended)...................................*
Avocado 1 piece soft / 300g. (recommended)........................... earth
Salt 1 pinch / 0,5g. (recommended)...water

Pepper (ground) 1 pinch / 0,2g. (little)..metal
Linseed oil 2 teaspoons / 4g. (recommended) .... earth

Cooking instructions:
Put quinoa in hot water.
Add grated carrot, pepper and salt, finely chopped spring onion and turmeric.
Simmer about 20 minutes, pull from the fire.
Add pre-cut avocado.
Add a dash of oil and sprinkle with fresh parsley.

Spices and herbs: turmeric, cardamom, cress, parsley, chives.

Variation: For those who want more hearty, you can also use a sardine from organic fish preserves. If you are the "protein type", this breakfast will hold on for a long time!

9.30 Quinoa with peach

Strengthens blood and fluids, brings blood into motion, builds up Qi, spreads, forces Qi, dries out, passes downwardly, strengthens middle heater, moisturizes.
Cooking time approx. 20 min
Calories p. portion: 248
2 portions

Quantity of ingredients
Quinoa 1 cup / 100g. (recommended) .... fire
Water 1 1/2 cups / 240g. (yes)... earth
Honey 2 teaspoons / 4g. .... earth
Peaches 2 pieces / 240g. (recommended)................................ earth
Linseed oil 2 teaspoons / 4g. (recommended) .... earth
Lemon Balm (fresh) 1 teaspoon / 1g. (recommended) ....metal
Cinnamon ground 1 pinch / 0,2g. (recommended) ....*
Vanilla 1 pinch / 0,2g. (yes) ....*

Cooking instructions:
In the evening: Put quinoa in hot water and boil soft, covered 15 to 20 minutes.
In the morning: Warm up quinoa with 1 tablespoon water.
Steam lightly Peaches in a saucepan or add them fresh. Decorate with fresh lemon balm.
Summer: nectarines, apricots - Winter: Pickled fruit, pear, apples

9.31 Red lentils with avocado and radish

Nutritious and moisturizing builds up Qi and fluids, drives sweat, reduces blood fat, stimulates, dissolves stagnation.
Cooking time approx. 20 min
Calories p. portion: 269
3 portions
Allergens: N

Quantity of ingredients
Ginger fresh 2 slices / 2g. (recommended) ....metal
Water 1 1/2 cups / 200g. (yes)... earth
Lentils red 1 cup peeled / 100g. (yes).......................................water
Wakame 1 inch / 1g. (recommended)..water
Salt 1 pinch / 0,5g. (recommended)..water
Lemon juice 1 dash / 1g. .... wood
Curcuma 1 pinch / 0,3g. (recommended)..*
Avocado 1 piece / 300g. (recommended) .... earth
Pepper (ground) 1 pinch / 0,2g. (little).....................................metal
Pepper powder (hot) 1 pinch / 0,2g. (recommended) .... fire
Sesame oil 1 dash / 1g. (yes).. earth
Radish (white, green, purple-red) 1 cup / 100g. (yes)................metal

Cooking instructions:
Put in a pot with water, some chopped ginger, peeled red lentils, a piece of wakame or a small amount of hijiki and simmer until the lentils are soft. Season with salt, lemon juice and turmeric.

Meanwhile: place half an avocado per serving on one-third of the plate: add ground pepper, a pinch of salt, a little lemon juice, a pinch of sweet pepper and a little sesame oil.

Put the grated radish on the second plate third.

Fill the lentil dish into the last third of the plate.
Variant: Use radish slices instead of radishes.

9.32 Reissue soup with fresh fruits

Forces kidney and bladder, strengthens Qi and kidney Jing, moisturizes, relaxes, builds up Qi, reduces internal heat, produces humors, moisturizes, spreads, expels cold, dissolves stagnation, drives sweat, stimulates nerves.

Cooking time approx. 1 1/2 hours
Calories p. portion: 143
4 portions
Allergens: G

Quantity of ingredients
Rice wild (nature rice) 1 cup / 100g. (yes)..................................metal
Water 8 cups / 900g. (yes) .... earth
Apple (sweet) 1 1/2 cups / 200g. (little).................................... earth
Butter organic 1 table spoon / 10g. (yes) .... earth
Vanilla 1 pinch / 0,2g. (yes) .... *
Sugar cane sugar 2 teaspoons / 6g. .... earth

Cooking instructions:
Prepare rice congee according to basic recipe.

At the end, add finely chopped fruits to the season, vanilla, chili and
butter; sweet to taste.

Variant: With nuts, the dish can always be made richer and more filling.

Effect: Cooked or steamed fruits are easier to digest and act better
than raw. For some fruits, which are particularly suitable for hot summer
days - such as melons and berries - it is still advisable to add the fruits
only to a hot porridge.
Other types of fruit - such as apples, pears, plums and cherries - can
also be simmered for a while.

9.33 Rice congee with carrots and fennel

Nutritious builds up Qi, forces the digestive functions.
Cooking time approx. 2 hours and more
Calories p. portion: 131
3 portions
Allergens: G

Quantity of ingredients
Basic recipe for a rice soup (Congee) 2 cup / 500g. (recommended) *
Carrot 2 pieces / 100g. (recommended).................................... earth
Fennel 1 piece / 250g. (yes)... earth
Butter organic 1 teaspoon / 3g. (yes)....................................... earth
Cardamom 1/2 teaspoon / 1g. (recommended)............................... *

Cooking instructions:
Cook rice congee according to basic recipe.
Clean and cut carrots and fennel.

When carrots and fennel are cooked from the beginning, they serve wholesomeness. If added shortly before the end of the cooking time, taste and vitamins are retained.

Refine with butter and cardamom before serving.

9.34 Rice congee with dried fruit

Warms the stomach and spleen, harmonizes the intestine, forces Qi, reduces moisture, nourishes blood and Yi, harmonizes lungs Qi, strengthens Qi and kidney Jing, moisturizes, relaxes, builds up Qi, spreads.
Cooking time approx. 10 min
Calories p. portion: 210
2 portions
Allergens: GO

Quantity of ingredients
Basic recipe for a rice soup (Congee) 4 cups / 500g. (recommended)*
Butter organic 1/2 teaspoon / 5g. (yes) .... earth
Apricot dried 6 table spoons / 50g. (recommended) .... earth
Water 1/2 cup / 50g. (yes) .... earth
Maple syrup 1 dash / 3g. (yes) .... earth

Cooking instructions:
Cook rice congee according to basic recipe.

Melt a small amount of butter over a low heat and briefly fry small dried fruit with 1/2 cup of water. Add the amount of rice porridge desired for the meal and heat. Serve hot and sweeten with maple syrup if necessary.
Variant: In addition fresh fruit with braise.

9.35 Rice dulse soup

Strengthens spleen and liver, regulates Qi flow, relaxes, builds up Qi, spreads, dries out, passes downwardly, strengthens stomach Qi, warms the stomach and spleen, harmonizes the intestine, forces Qi, reduces moisture.
Cooking time approx. 5 min
Calories p. portion: 190
2 portions
Allergens: L

Quantity of ingredients
Basic recipe for a rice soup (Congee) 4 cups / 500g. (recommended)*
Basic recipe for a vegetable soup (nutritious) 2 cup / 500g. (recommended)*
Dulse (seaweed) 2 table spoons / 15g. (recommended) ....water

Cooking instructions:
Worm up a portion of pre-cooked basic recipe for a ricesoupe (congee) and a portion pre-cooked basic recipe for a vegetable soup.
Bake the dulse in the oven at 220 degrees for 3 minutes. Spread the crisp dulse over the rice.

9.36 Rice noodle soup with shiitake mushrooms

Strengthens spleen and liver, regulates Qi flow, relaxes, builds up Qi, spreads, dries out, passes downwardly, strengthens stomach Qi, nourishes Yin of the lungs, stomach and colon, supports digestion, reduces internal wind.
Cooking time approx. 20 min
Calories p. portion: 66
2 portions
Allergens: L

Quantity of ingredients
Rice noodles 2 handful / 20g. (yes) ....metal
Shiitake, dried 4-6 pieces / 5g. (recommended).........................earth
Basic recipe for a vegetable soup 1 1/2 cups / 240g. (recommended)*
Chinese cabbage 1 cup / 60g. (recommended)..........................earth
Lovage 1 teaspoon / 3g. (yes) ....metal
Miso 2 table spoons / 18g. (yes)..water

Cooking instructions:
Soak rice noodles and shiitake mushrooms separately in cold water.
Heat the vegetable broth and add the soaked shiitake mushrooms cut
into strips and simmer gently. Cut Chinese cabbage into noodles, add
lovage green and rice noodles and let it steep for a while. Before
serving, stir in Miso dissolved in a little cooled water. Recommendation:
Suitable at the beginning of each meal, also for breakfast

9.37 Rice soup with grated carrots and fresh herbs

Strengthens spleen and liver, regulates Qi flow, moisturizes, relaxes,
builds up Qi, spreads, forces kidney and bladder.
Cooking time approx. 5 min
Calories p. portion: 131
4 portions
Allergens: EG

Quantity of ingredients
Rice wild (nature rice) 1 cup / 100g. (yes)..................................metal
Water 6 cups / 700g. (yes) .... earth
Carrot 1 piece / 100g. (recommended) .... earth
Soy sauce 1 dash / 2g. ....water
Butter organic 1 teaspoon / 3g. (yes).. earth
Ground 1 pinch / 0,3g. (recommended) .... earth
Curcuma 1 pinch / 0,2g. (recommended).......................................*
Herbs various 1 teaspoon (chopped) / 3g. (recommended)..............*

Cooking instructions:
In a portion of rice congee according to basic recipe, softly cook a
grated carrot, add butter and soy sauce.
Sprinkle with fresh herbs.

Spices and herbs: black cumin, turmeric, cardamom, parsley, sage,
thyme, basil, rosemary.

Winter: parsnip, celery, onion, leek, pumpkin
Summer: tomatoes, zucchini, spring onion, radishes, arugula.

9.38 Roasted oatmeal with grapes compote

Moisturizes, relaxes, builds up Qi, spreads, forces Qi, warms the stomach and spleen, promotes blood circulation and conduction flow.
Cooking time approx. 25 min
Calories p. portion: 328
2 portions
Allergens: AO

Quantity of ingredients
Oat flakes roasted 1 cup / 120g. (recommended) ....metal
Grapes red 1 1/2 cups / 240g. (yes)... earth
Ginger fresh 1/2 teaspoon / 1g. (recommended).......................metal
Raisins 2 table spoons / 20g. (recommended)........................... earth
Cinnamon ground 1 pinch / 1g. (recommended) ....*
Water 1 1/2 cups / 200g. (yes).. earth

Cooking instructions:
Roast the oats briefly, pour over water, add raisins and cook while stirring for 20 min. Add grapes, ginger and cinnamon.

9.39 Spelled-grid porridge with berries of the season

Nourishes fluids, moisturises dryness, produces humors, moisturizes intestines, cools inner heat, preserves the fluids, contracts, forces middle, nourishes heart and liver-blood, preserves the fluids, contracts.
Cooking time approx. 15 min
Calories p. portion: 244
2 portions
Allergens: AGH

Quantity of ingredients
Cow's milk (1.5% fat) 1/2 cup / 125g. (little) ....*
Water 1/2 cup / 125g. (yes) .... earth
Spelled semolina 5 table spoons / 50g. (yes)............................ wood
Butter organic 2 teaspoons / 20g. (yes) .... earth
Berries of the season 1/4 lbs - 4oz / 100g. (recommended) .... wood
Honey 1-2 teaspoons / 5g. .... earth
Almond 1-2 teaspoons / 5g. (yes)... earth
Peppermint 3-4 leaves / 2g. (recommended) ....metal
Cinnamon ground 1 pinch / 0,5g. (recommended) ....*
Vanilla 1 pinch / 0,2g. (yes) ....*
Cocoa 1 pinch / 0,5g. (recommended).. fire
Coconut grated 1 table spoon / 10g. (yes) .... earth

Cooking instructions:
Stir in spelled semolina in cold water and boil slowly over medium heat. After boiling, remove from the heat and let simmer for a few minutes. Depending on the desired consistency, some water may have to be added. Stir in the butter and fine grated nuts in the mash and raspberries. Serve with honey or whole-grain sugar as desired.
Spices and aromas: fresh mint, cinnamon or vanilla, cocoa, coconut

Summer: raspberries, blueberries, strawberries

9.40 Sweet polenta with peach

Nourishing and warming, harmonizes the middle.
Cooking time approx. 20 min
Calories p. portion: 330
2 portions
Allergens: GHO

Quantity of ingredients
Water 1 1/2 cups / 240g. (yes).. earth
Corn Grease (Polenta) 1 cup / 100g. (yes) .... earth
Butter organic 1/2 teaspoon / 2g. (yes)...................................... earth
Barley malt 1/2 teaspoon / 2g. (recommended)......................... earth
Cinnamon ground 1 pinch / 0,2g. (recommended) .... *
Cardamom 1 pinch / 0,2g. (recommended)................................... *
Salt 1 pinch / 0,5g. (recommended)..water
Lemon 1 dash / 1g. .... wood
Raisins 2 table spoons / 20g. (recommended).......................... earth
Apple juice (natural cloudy) until covered / 10g. (little) .... earth
Peaches 2 pieces / 240g. (recommended)................................ earth
Hazelnuts 2 table spoons / 20g. (yes)..................................... earth

Cooking instructions:
Heat water till it boils. Stir in the polenta with a whisk and until tender; add some butter or cream, barley malt or maple syrup, cinnamon, some cardamom, a pinch of salt, a few drops of lemon juice and stir well.

Separately prepare a compote:
In a hot pot, simmer raisins in some apple or apricot juice for a few minutes; add fully ripe peaches chopped and heat; pour over the polenta served on plates; sprinkle with roasted nuts as desired.

9.41 Tea from ginseng

Forces heart, lungs, stomach, spleen, kidney-Qi.
Cooking time approx. 20 min
Calories p. portion: 0
4 portions

Quantity of ingredients
Ginseng 2 teabags / 4g. (recommended)..*
Water 2 cup / 500g. (yes) .... earth

Cooking instructions:
A very mild form of taking ginseng is achieved by placing it in a thermos
of hot water. You can also use the root several times, not just for a pot
filling. Ideally, you should have cooked the water for 10 minutes - it is
then assigned to the conversion phase of fire (TCM) - and to use non-
carbonated medicinal spring water, if the quality of the water on site is
not good.

Ingestion: This mild ginseng tea can be drunk throughout the day for
strengthening.

9.42 Tea from juniper berry

Dries out, passes downwardly, activates Wei Qi.
Cooking time approx. 10 min
Calories p. portion: 10
1 portions

Quantity of ingredients
Juniper berry 1 teaspoon / 3g. (recommended)............................ fire
Water 1 cup / 125g. (yes) .... earth

Cooking instructions:
A teaspoon of dried juniper berries for a cup of tea. Start cold and bring
to the boil. Let it sit for 15 minutes, then strain.
This tea is unsweetened and swallowed, slowly drunk. The amount is
enough for one day.

9.43 Tea from Longane

Forces spleen, builds up lung, builds up heart, calms nerves.
Cooking time approx. 10 min
Calories p. portion: 0
4 portions

Quantity of ingredients
Longane 2 teaspoons / 4g. (recommended)......................................*
Water 2 cup / 500g. (yes)... earth

Cooking instructions:
Heat the water till it boils and put it aside. Add Longane and 10 min. to
let go. Sweet to taste with honey. Strain when pouring.

9.44 Tea from rosemary

Dries out, passes downwardly, forces heart, lung and spleen Qi, forces
liver-blood, forces heart-Yin, expels spleen heat / cold moisture,
strengthens spleen and kidney Yang.
Cooking time approx. 15 min
Calories p. portion: 1
4 portions

Quantity of ingredients
Rosemary 2-4 teaspoons / 6g. (recommended) .... fire
Water 2 cup / 500g. (yes)... earth

Cooking instructions:
Heat the water till it boils and put it aside. Add rosemary and 10 min. to
let go. Strain. Sweet to taste with honey.

9.45 Warming porridge

Forces Qi and defensive power.
Cooking time approx. 10 min
Calories p. portion: 357
1 portions
Allergens: AHO

Quantity of ingredients

Oat flakes (whole grain) 6 table spoons / 60g. (yes)...................metal
Fig dried 3 pieces / 15g. (yes) .... earth
Star anise 1 piece / 1g. (yes).. *
Ginger fresh 1 pinch / 0,5g. (recommended)............................metal
Water 1 cup / 120g. (yes)... earth
Maple syrup 1 table spoon / 10g. (yes).................................... earth
Walnuts 1 table spoon (chopped) / 8g. (recommended)............. earth

Cooking instructions:

Soak the dried fruit. Roast Oatmeal dry. Add dried ginger, star anise or cinnamon, a little grated ginger and boil everything with water to a mash. With maple syrup sweet. Whip grated walnuts and sprinkle before serving.

Effect: Suitable for the cold season.
Caution: Fresh ginger does not drink over a long period of time.

10 Effects of food

10.1 Use ingredients: recommendable

Acai powder
Acerola fruit nectar or powder
Agar agar (kelp)
Agave nectar
Agrimony
Aloe juice
Amaranth
Amaranth Pops
Angelica root
Apple (sour)
Apple puree
Apricot dried
Apricot jam
Apricot nectar
Apricots juice
Aubergine
Avocado
Baking powder
Balm
Bamboo shoots
Banchatee (green tea)
barberry
Barley flour
Barley grass powder
Barley grouts
Barley malt
Barley not peeled
Basic recipe for a beef soup
Basic recipe for a beef soup (warming)
Basic recipe for a chicken soup (warming)
Basic recipe for a duck soup
Basic recipe for a fish soup
Basic recipe for a rice soup (Congee)
Basic recipe for a vegetable soup (nutritious)
Batavia
Bay leaf
Beans (green, fresh)
Bearberry leaf
Beef bone marrow
Beef heart
Beef heart (calf)
Beef kidney
Beef liver
Beef lungs (calf)
Beef Oxtail pieces
Beef soup meat
Beef stomach

Beer (alcohol-free)
Beer (alcohol-reduced)
Berries of the season
Bitter Herb liqueur
Bitter Lemon
Bitter liqueur
Bitter orange peel
Black beans
Black caraway
Black fungus mushroom
Blackberry dried (unripe fruit)
Blackberry jam
Blackberry leaves
Blackberry´s
Blackthorn (Sloe)
Blue mallow tee
Blueberry dried
Blueberry jam
Boletus mushroom
Borage
 Borage oil
Boxhorn clover seeds
Brazil nuts
Bread roll
Bread with carob kernel flour
Breadcrumbs (wheat bread, bread roll)
Brie cheese
Broccoli
Brown ale
Brussels sprouts
Buckbean
Buckwheat
Buckwheat (roasted) Kasha
Buckwheat whole grain
Butter (half fat)
Buttermilk
Camembert
Campari
Capers in olive oil
Cardamom
Carob flour, St. john's bread
Carrot
Carrot (Early Carrot)
Carrot juice without sugar
Cauliflower
Celery root
Cereal coffee
Chamomile
Chamomile tea

Champignon
Channa-Dal
Chanterelle
Chenpi (chinese tangerine bowl)
Cherry
Cherry (sour)
Cherry compote
Chervil
Chervil dried
Chestnut puree
Chicken Blood
Chicken egg
Chicken egg white
Chicken liver
Chicken stomach
Chicken yolk
Chickpeas
Chickweed
Chili (pod or ground)
Chinese cabbage
Chinese pearl barley
Chlorella (fresh water)
Chocolate
Chocolate (Diabetic)
Chrysanthemum blossom tea
Cinnamon ground
Cinnamon sticks
Clarified butter
Clementine
Clementines
Cocoa
Coconut fat
Coconut meat
Codfish
Coix (seeds) YiYi Ren
Cola drink
Cola drink (low calorie)
Compote (fruits of the season)
Cooking oil
Coriander (fresh)
Corn
Corn (fast polenta)
Corn flour
Corn germ oil
Corn silk tea
Corn starch
Cottage cheese
Cranberries
Cranberry
Cranberry jam
Cream (30% fat)
Cream 10% coffee cream
Cream sour 10%
Cream sour 20%

Cream sour 30%
Cream, sweet 30%
Creamer
Créme fraiche cheese
Crispbread
Cucumber (bitter)
Cucumber (spicy cucumber)
Curcuma
Curd cheese 20%
Curd cheese 40%
Currant (black)
Currant (red)
Currant (white)
Currant jam (black)
Currant jam (red)
Currant juice (black)
Currants (black)
Currants (red)
Curry paste red
Daisy
Dandelion juice
Dashi
Dates red
Deer meat
Deer meat
Deer's Bones
Deer's kidneys
Ducks egg
Dulse (seaweed)
Dyer's broom herb
Edam cheese
Eel smoked
Elderberries
Emmental cheese
Evening primrose oil
Fennel seeds ground
Fenugreek (Trigonella foenum-graecum)
Fernet Branca (herbal bitter liqueur)
Feta cheese
Feta cheese
Fish innards
Fish remains
Fish sauce
Flounder
Flower pollen
Fox nut, gorgon nut, makhana
Fresh cheese
Fresh cheese from soya
Fresh cheese with herbs
Freshwater crab
Freshwater fish
Fructose (glucose)
Fruit mix juice

Fruit tea
Gail plum
Galangal
Garam Masala powder
Garlic
Gelatin white
Gelee Royal
Gentian root
Gentian root tea
Ginger fresh
Ginger oil
Ginkgo fruit
Ginseng
Ginseng liqueur
Ginseng root
Goat
Goat and sheep's blood
Goat and sheep's brain
Goat and sheep's liver
Goat and sheep's milk
Goat and sheep's stomach
Goat cheese
Goose blood
Goose egg
Goose fat
Gorgonzola
Gouda cheese
Grapefruit dried peel
Grapeseed oil
Greengage
Ground
Ground caraway
Guava
Halibut (Flatfish)
Herbal tea mix
Herbs bitter
Herbs of Provence
Herbs various
Herbs wild
Hibiscus
Hibiscus tea
Hijiki
Hokkaido pumpkin
Honey wine (Met)
Hop
Horehound leaves
Horse meat
Jasmine blossoms tee
Jellyfish
Juniper berry
Kaki plum
Kalmus
Kefir
King Solomon's-seal

Kohlrabi
Kombu seaweed (Saccharina japonica)
Kudzu
Kukicha tea
Ladyfingers
Lamb kidneys
Lamb liver
Lamb's lettuce
Lavender blossoms
Leek
Lemon Balm (dried)
Lemon Balm (fresh)
Lemongrass
Licorice root tea
Lily bulbs
Lime blossom tea
Linseed
Linseed (crushed)
Linseed oil
Liver smoothing tea
Lobster
Longane
Loquate / Japanese medlar
Lotus roots
Lotus seeds
Lovage seeds
Luo Han Guo fruit
Lychee
Lychee in Preserved
Lychee liqueur
Lye roll
Mackerel
Mallow (Malva sylvestris) blossom tea
Malt
Mango juice
Manioc flour
Mare's milk
Marjoram
Martini
Mascarpone cheese
Mayonnaise 50%
Mayonnaise 80%
Mediterranean fish (cod, plaice, haddock, sea eel, mackerel)
Medlar
Mineral water
Mirabelle plum
Miso black (fermented)
Mixed Pickles
Morel, dried
Mu Erh Mushroom
Muesli
Mulled Wine Spice
Multi-grain bread (gray bread)

Mustard
Mustard Dijon
Mustard medium hot
Mustard sweet
Mutton
Mutton
Nasturtium (nose-twister or nose-tweaker)
Nectarine
Nettles
Noodles (wheat) with egg
Noodles (wheat, lasagne) with egg
Noodles (wheat, ribbon noodles) with egg
Noodles (wheat, spaghetti) with egg
Noodles (whole grain) with egg
Nori, purple seaweed, red algae
Nutmeg
Oat
Oat flakes roasted
Octopus
Olives green
Orange blossom
Orange dried peel
Orange grated peel
Orange jam
Orange peel
Oregano dried
Oregano fresh
Oyster mushroom
Oyster shell powder
Palm oil
Parsley root
Parsnip
Passion blossoms tea
Passion fruit
Peaches
Peaches (canned)
Peanut (roasted)
Peanut butter
Pear
Pear juice
Pearl barley
Pearl barley
Pepper powder (hot)
Peppermint
Peppermint tea
Pepperoni
Pepperoni, red, pitted, halved
Pepperoni, yellow, pitted, halved
Peppers (rose peppers)
Peppers (sweet)
Peppers powder
Pickle

Pig blood
Pigeon
Pigeon egg
Pineapple
Pineapple (from a can)
Pineapple juice without sugar
Pinto beans speckled
Pistachios
Plum dried
Plums
Poppy
Pork Bacon
Pork brain
Pork fat (lard)
Pork ham
Pork ham cooked
Pork ham smoked
Pork heart
Pork kidneys
Pork knuckle
Pork Lard
Pork liver
Pork lung
Pork marrow bones
Pork meat
Pork sausage (Bratwurst) Pork skin
Pork stomach
Pork/beef sausage (smoked)
Pork's intestine
Potato (mealy)
Potato flour
Prickly pear
Processed cheese 12%
processed cheese 30%
Prosecco
Psyllium seed
Pudding powder vanilla
Puff pastry
Pumpernickel (dark bread)
Quail
Quail egg
Quinoa
Rabbit (wild)
Radish horseradish
Radish leaves
Raisins
Raspberry
Raspberry dried (immature)
Raspberry jam
Raspberry leaf tea
Red beet
Red cabbage
Reishi mushroom
Ribworttea

Rice (fragrance)
Rice (Gaoliang / Sorghum)
Rice Basmati
Rice mash
Rice starch
Rice sticky
Rose blossom tea
Rose hip
Rose leaf tea
Rosefish
Rosemary
Rum
Rusk
Rye wholemeal bread
Safflower (Dyer's thistle / Hong Hua)
Sage
Sake
Salt
Salt (herbal)
Sauerkraut (cutted cabbage fermented)
Savoy cabbage / kale
Sea buckthorn
Sea cucumber
Sesame oil roasted
Sesame paste (Tahini)
Sesame, black
Sesame, white
Sheep's milk
Sheep's milk yoghurt
Sherry (whine)
Shiitake, dried
Shrimps
Skim milk powder
Slug
Sour cherries
Sour cream 15% fat
Sour milk
Sourdough
Soy flour
Soy noodles
Soy Tofu smoked
Soya Cuisine (soy cream)
Soybeans
Soybeans, blacks, fermented
Spelled flakes
Spinach
Spirit
Spurdog (spiny dogfish, Schillerlocken)
St. Benedict's thistle, blessed thistle,
holy thistle, spotted thistle
Stevia (candyleaf, sweetleaf)
Strawberry jam
Sugar - icing sugar
Sugar molasses

Sugar palm sugar
Sugar substitute (sweetener)
Supplementary nutrition
Sweet potato
Tabasco
Tangerine
Tea mixture uric acid lowering
Thistle oil
Thyme dried
Toast bread (whole grain)
Tomato dried
Tomato juice
Tomato paste
Tomato puree
Tonic Water
Topinambur
Trout (smoked)
Truffle
Tsampa (roasted barley flour)
Turkey ham
Turmeric (yellow root)
Turnip
Turnips
Umeboshi paste
Valerian
Vanilla pod
Vanilla sugar natural
Vinegar (Red wine vinegar)
Vinegar Aceto Balsamico
Vinegar Aceto Balsamico white
Wakame
Walnut oil
Walnuts
Walnuts roasted
Water hot
Wax gourd
Wheat flatbread/pita bread
Wheat flour whole grain
Wheat/Rye/Gray-black bread with yeast
Wheatgrass juice
Wheatgrass powder
Whey
White bread (baguette)
White bread (pretzel sticks)
White bread (roll)
White bread (wheat bread)
White breadcrumbs
White cabbage
White dumpling bread (wheat bread cut
into chunks)
White wine
Whitefish
Whole grain bread
Wholemeal flour

Wild boar meat
Wild garlic (garlic spinach)
Wild herbs
Wild strawberries
Wormwood
Wormwood herb

Yam root, yam root tuber
Yarrow
Yeast
Yew nut
Yoghurt vanilla

10.2 Use ingredients: yes

Adzuki beans
Almond
Almond marzipan
Almond milk
Almond puree
Anchovy / Sardine
Anise (Common Fennel)
Apricot
Apricots
Arrowroot
Artichoke
Barley
Basil
Basil (fresh)
Bean oil
Beef fillet
Beef meat
Beef meat (calf)
Beef meatbones
Beer (Pils)
Beer (Top-fermented German dark beer)
Berry juice
Black-eyed peas
Blueberry
Blueberry juice
Bocksdorn fruits (Fructus Lycii, Goji, goji berry dried)
Broad beans (thick beans)
Bush beans
Butter beans white
Butter organic
Calamari
Carp
Cashews
Celery sticks
Cherry juice
Chestnuts
Chicken heart
Chicken meat
Chicory
Chives
Clove
Coconut flakes
Coconut grated

Coconut milk
Cod
Coriander
Corn (roasted)
Corn Grease (Polenta)
Cranberry
Cranberry juice
Crucian
Cumin (Caraway seed)
Dates dried
Dill
Duck (heart)
Eel
Elderberry blossom tee
Fennel
Fennel tea
Fig
Fig dried
Fish pieces mixed (fresh water)
French beans
Goose
Goose parts
Gooseberry
Gourd
Grape juice red
Grape juice white
Grapes red
Grapes white
Grass carp
Green spelt
Hawthorn
Hazelnuts
Herring
Hyssop
Kidney beans (red)
Kumquats
Leaf salads (bitter)
Lentils
Lentils black
Lentils red
Lentils yellow
Lima beans
Lovage
Maple syrup
Margarine

Margarine (diet)
Millet
Millet flakes
Miso
Morel (black, dried)
Mulberry fruit
Mung bean
Mustard seeds
Oat flakes (whole grain)
Oat flour
Oat fusion (baby food)
Oat meal
Oat milk
Octopus
Okra
Olive oil
Olives
Onion (shallot)
Onion (spring onion)
Onion read
Onion white
Oysters
Parsley
Peanut oil
Peanuts
Peas
Peas, green
Peppers
Perch
Pheasant
Pine nuts
Plaice
Plum
Pomegranate
Potato
Pumpkin
Pumpkin seed oil
Pumpkin seeds
Quince
Rabbit
Rabbit meat
Radish
Radish (white, green, purple-red)
Radish black
Rapeseed oil
Red berry (without sugar)
Rice (whole grain)
Rice black
Rice flour

Rice long grain rice
Rice malt
Rice noodles
Rice red
Rice round grain
Rice sweet
Rice variety any
Rice wild (nature rice)
Rucola
Rye
Rye flour
Saffron
Sago (cereals)
Salmon
Salsify
Savory
Sesame oil
Shark
Shrimp
Sour milk cheese 20%
Soy Tofu
Soybean milk
Soybean oil
Soybeans, black
Soybeans, yellow
Spelled (Dark) bread
Spelled grain
Spelled semolina
Spelled wholemeal flour
Spiny lobsters
Star anise
Strawberries
Strawberry Juice
Sunflower oil
Sunflower seeds
Tarragon (Estragon)
Thyme
Trout
Tuna
Turkey breast meat
Umeboshi plums (Japanese apricots)
Vanilla
Vanilla powder
Vinegar (Apple vinegar)
Water
Wheat germ oil
White beans
Zucchini

10.3 Use ingredients: little

Apple (sweet)

Apple juice (natural cloudy)

Bulgur (cereals)
Coffee
Couscous
Cow's milk (1.5% fat)
Cow's milk (whole milk 3.5% fat)
Duck (slaughtered)
Endive salad
Iceberg lettuce
Lettuce
Mozzarella
Parmesan
Pepper (ground)
Pepper Cayenne
Pepper white (ground)
Peppercorns
Radicchio
Red wine
Romaine lettuce / lettuce salad
Wheat
Wheat bulgur
Wheat flakes
Wheat flour
Wheat semolina
Wheat semolina for children

10.4 Do not use contra-acting foods

Asparagus (green or white)
Banana
Banana (cooking banana)
Black tea
Burdock root tea
Cantaloupe
Carambola (Star fruit)
Caviar
Chard
Crab
Cress
Cucumber
Curry
Dandelion (young plants)
Dandelionroots tea
Ginger powder
Grapefruit (Pomelo)
Grapefruit juice
Green tea
Honey
Kiwi
Lamb bones
Lamb meat
Lamb shoulder
Lamb's lettuce
Lemon
Lemon juice
Lemon peel
Lime
Mango
Miso paste (soy bean paste)
Mold cheese
Mullet
Mung bean sprouting
Mussels
Orange
Orange juice
Papaya
Pimento
Rabbit liver
Rhubarb
Rose hip tea
Seacrab
Sorrel
Soy sauce
Sugar brown
Sugar candy white
Sugar cane sugar
Sugar fructose - fruit sugar
Sugar glucose - grapes sugar
Sugar Milk Sugar
Sugar white
Tomato
Vegetable juice
Watermelon
Wheat beer
Wheat bran
Yarrow tea
Yogi tea
Yogurt (natural, 1.5% fat)
Yogurt (natural, 3.5% fat)

11 Herbs and their effects

11.1 Basil

thermal effect: warm
taste: spicy, bitter
Dries out, leads down. Tonifies Yang and Qi, dissolves mucus-cold, eliminates wind-cold.
It has a beneficial effect on flatulence and nausea, relaxing and soothing. Good to fight emphysema, bronchitis, whooping cough, high blood pressure, headache, mouth odor, warts, hiccup, gout, migraine.

11.2 Mugwort

thermal effect: warm
taste: bitter, spicy
Regulates and nourishes bleeding, warms the inside, eliminates wind-cold, eliminates parasites, eliminates heat, wetness, regulates and moves Qi.
Reduces bleeding, alleviates pain. In the kitchen, mugwort is used as a spice for fat food. Since it contains many bitter substances, it boosts fat burning and promotes digestion.

11.3 Savory

thermal effect: warm
taste: bitter
Tonifies kidney yang, heart qi, stomach and spleen qi and warms the middle, moves the liver qi and blood, releases mucous and cold from the lungs, opens the surface, induces wind-cold.
Stomach-strengthening, soothing and appetizing. Ideal for prevent colds, strengthens the immune system. In case of incontinence or nocturnal wetting (not for children), put the beans in liquor for libido.

11.4 Coriander

thermal effect: warm
taste: spicy
Driving sweat, reducing wind, draining moisture, tonifying and regulating qi, eliminating wind-cold.
The essential oils are appetizing, digestive, cramping and soothing in stomach and intestinal disorders.

11.5 Herbs various

Stimulates appetite. Effect different.
Appetizing, lots of trace elements and vitamins.

11.6 Chives

thermal effect: warm
taste: spicy
Directs upward. Tonifies blood, kidney Yang and Qi. Dissolves moisture.
Bactericide, prevents cancer, strengthens gastric juice production,
promotes digestion and blood circulation, promotes growth, triggers
stagnation.

11.7 Lovage

thermal effect: warm
taste: spicy, bitter
Reduces inner wind and moisture, dissolves stagnation, directs upward,
warms Yang, regulates and moves Qi, warms inside, dissolves mucus-
cold, eliminates wind-cold.
Stimulates digestion, reduces pain. Extracts of the root are used to flush
out urinary tract infections and prevent kidney gravel.

11.8 Lily bulbs

thermal effect: cool
taste: sweet, bitter
Tonifies Yin, soothes Shen / Spirit. Moisturizes the lungs, clears heat and
stops coughing.
Calms nerves, good to fight scaly skin. The onions and the petals are
added to ointments in the Orient, which can heal muscles and tendons.
White lily (astringent).

11.9 Oregano fresh

thermal effect: warm
taste: bitter
Dries out, directs down, regulates and moves Qi, eliminates wind-cold,
soothes Shen / Spirit, suppresses inner wind, warms inside, eliminates
wind-cold / heat-wetness, moves blood, dissolves slime-cold.
It has an anti-digestive, calming and nerve-strengthening effect, helps to
fight cramping stomach and intestinal disorders. The ingredient Carvacrol
has an anti-inflammatory effect.

11.10 Parsley

thermal effect: warm
taste: bitter
Nourishes blood and liver, harmonizes liver and spleen, strengthens eyesight, preserves juices, contracts. Dissolves moisture and warms Yang.
Stimulates liver function, detoxifies. Forces urinating. Relieves flatulence. Digestive and menstrual stimulating, birth-accelerating, memory-enhancing, blood-purifying, skin-smoothing.

11.11 Peppermint

thermal effect: cool
taste:spicy, bitter
Cools heat, expels mucus, dissipates wind-cold and wind-heat, moves stomach qi, releases congestion, tonifies, regulates and moves qi.
Relaxes, frees the lungs and the nose (inhale), regulates the cycle.
Stimulates bile flow and bile production, antispasmodic in gastrointestinal disorders, antimicrobial and antiviral.

11.12 Rosemary

thermal effect: warm
taste: bitter
Dries out, leads down. Strengthens the heart, lungs and spleen qi, strengthens liver blood. Strengthens heart-Yin. Expels spleen heat / cold moisture. Strengthens spleen and kidney yang.
Promotes digestion, relieves bloating, strengthens lung, spleen and kidney. Affects the circulation and nerves. Appetizing. Baths help to fight circulatory disorders as well as with gout and rheumatism.

11.13 Sage

thermal effect: neutral
taste:bitter, spicy
Expels slime, guides down, strengthens Qi, eliminates Wind-Heat, eliminate heat induced by Yin deficiency.
Good to fight yeast infections. The leaves have a digestive effect and are used in greasy foods. Antiperspirant effect. Helps to relieve coughing attacks. Dries out.

11.14 Black caraway

thermal effect: warm
taste: spicy, sweet
Dissolve / transform moisture, tonifies Yang and Qi, moves blood, suppresses inner wind. Detoxifying, immunoregulatory. In addition, the oil should stimulate the formation of bone marrow cells and generally protect body cells from viruses.

11.15 King Solomon's-seal

thermal effect: neutral
taste:sweet, bitter
Tonifies Yin and Qi, astringent, tonifies blood, eliminates wind-cold / heat-wetness. Used to repair wounds or damaged tissue. Good to fight dry cough, earlier also tuberculosis and dysentery, as well as diarrhea and hemorrhoids.

11.16 Yam root, yam root tuber

thermal effect: neutral
taste:sweet
Tonifies Yin, Yang and Qi, reduces inner wind, dissolves wetness, warms Yang. Solves cramps (in the gastrointestinal tract). Digestive through increased bile production. Anti-inflammatory in rheumatic diseases. Mucolytic agent for coughing. Relief of menopausal symptoms.

11.17 Lemongrass

thermal effect: taste:
Diverting, calming.
Reduction of flatulence, antimicrobial, appetizing. Prevention of influenza. Good to fight infections in the mouth and throat.

11.18 Lemon Balm (fresh)

thermal effect: cool
taste:sour
Soothes Shen / Spirit, regulates and moves Qi, eliminates heat caused by Yin deficiency, tones Qi.
Stimulating, antibacterial, encouraging, relaxing, antispasmodic, cooling, antipyretic, analgesic, sweat-inducing, virus-inhibiting. Good for colds, fever, flu, cough, bronchitis, asthma, loss of appetite, bloating, heartburn.

12 Basics of Nutrition

The basic principles of nutrition described herein are general recommendations. They are not aimed at a specific form of therapy. Recommendations concerning a therapy have priority.

12.1 Nutrition

Regular meals in a relaxed atmosphere. A warm breakfast is considered a good start into the day.
The main meals ought to be taken for lunch – supper in the early evening. Pay attention to feeling hungry or sated: don't eat too much nor remain hungry is the rule
Prepare the meals freshly from natural, regional products. Frozen, heat-conserved, industrially prepared or foodstuffs cooked in the microwave oven are rejected.
Choice of foodstuffs according to the season: more cooling food in summer, more warming food in winter.
Eat cooked food at least twice a day. Food and drinks ought to be lukewarm, never ice-cold or hot.
Raw vegetables, briefly cooked vegetables, freshly squeezed juices and mineral water are not recommended. Milk and dairy products are only included in the diet if they don't cause problems. Don't use therapeutic recipes over a longer period without consulting your doctor or therapist.

Varied food
Enjoy the diversity of foodstuffs. Characteristics of a balanced nutrition are variety, suitable combination and a balanced quantity of rich and low energy foodstuffs (on one hand avoiding undersupply with essential nutrients and on the other hand to take to many undesirable substances).

A lot of Cereal Products - and Potatoes
Bread, pasta, rice, cereal flakes (best wholemeal) as well as potatoes contain almost no fat, but many vitamins, mineral nutrients, trace elements, roughage and secondary plant substances. These foodstuffs ought to be taken with low-fat side dishes.

Vegetables and Fruit – „Take Five" every day ... 5 portions of vegetables and fruit a day, as fresh as possible, briefly cooked, or maybe one portion as a juice – ideal as a side dish to every meal as well as snack between meals: Thus a lot of vitamins, mineral nutrients as well as roughage and secondary plant substances

Daily milk and dairy products
Milk and Dairy Products every Day, once or twice per Week Fish;
meat, sausages as well as eggs moderately. These foodstuffs contain
valuable nutrients like calcium in the milk, iodine selenium and omega-3
fat acids in saltwater fish. Meat is favorable due to its high content of
disposable iron and the vitamins B1, B6 and B12. Quantities of 300 – 600
g meat and sausage per week are sufficient. Prefer low-fat products,
especially in meat- and dairy products.

Low-fat and fatty Foodstuffs
Fat supplies us with essential fat acids and fatty foodstuffs contain also
fat-soluble vitamins. Fat is high in energy; therefore much fat in the food
may cause overweight, possibly also cancer. Too many saturated fat
acids may further a tendency for cardio-vascular diseases in the long
term. Prefer vegetable oils and fats (e.g. rapeseed-, olive-, soya-oils and
solid fats produced therefrom). Beware of invisible fat in meat- and dairy
products, pastry and sweets as well as in fast-food and convenience
foods. 70 – 90 g fat per day is sufficient.

Moderately Sugar and Salt
Take sugar and foods/drinks containing various kinds of sugar (e.g.
glucose syrup) only occasionally. Use herbs and spices as well as a little
salt creatively. Prefer salt containing iodine.

Plenty of Liquids
Water is absolutely essential. Drink 1-2 l liquids every day. Prefer water
(with or without gas) and other low-calorie drinks. Alcoholic drinks should
not be taken.

Tasty Dishes, carefully cooked
Cook the meals with as low temperatures and as short as possible, using
little water and fat – this preserves the original taste, keeps the nutrients
intact and prevents the production of harmful compounds.

Take time and enjoy the food
Take your Time and enjoy your Food
Eating consciously helps to eat right. The eye enjoys food, too. It's fun,
invites to enjoy varied dishes and stimulates the feeling of satiety.

Watch your Weight and stay in Motion
A balanced diet and a lot of exercise and sport (30 – 60 min/day) are a
healthy combination. The right weight furthers well-being and health.
Thermals, directional effectiveness, digestive power

There are various criteria for judging the effectiveness of herbs and foodstuffs.

The use of certain herbs and ingredients is based on observations of the effects on the body which these foodstuffs, herbs and spices show after having eaten them. The medical science has developed following system: Every ingredient or herb has a directional effectiveness. Furthermore, there are herbs which have a special effect on certain organs.

The basic condition for a healthy metabolism is to obtain sufficient energy from food and that the digestive process doesn't use too much energy. An easily digestible meal makes content and sated, doesn't cause flatulence and fatigue after the meal. The perfect spices increase the healthiness of our meals. Very often, just small doses of herbs and spices will suffice. They are not used to make us sated, but to help our digestive organs to digest the food.

12.2 Recipes

The recipes list the ingredients to be used and the cooking instructions show how the dish is prepared. The list of ingredients shows the concerned quantities as well as the relevance for the therapy. If you find „less than mentioned", try to comply or find an alternative from the „list of recommended foodstuffs". Mostly it shall result just in a small change of taste when you simply avoid this ingredient.

Mild cooking methods: boiling, stewing, poaching, steaming
Strong cooking methods: barbecuing, roasting, frying, smoking
Balanced cooking methods: deep-frying, baking brick
Deep-freezing and warming in the microwave oven should be avoided (denaturalization).

12.3 Foodstuffs

Foodstuffs have an effect on body and soul like medicinal herbs, only a very much milder one. Dietary advice is mainly based on regional foodstuffs. The knowledge about the effects of each foodstuff and the knowledge, when which foodstuff shall be used, is based on the orthodox school of medicine. Use ecologic-organic products, if possible. As everything should be cooked for a long time due to a better digestability and very rarely eaten raw, the food agrees with everyone.

The classification of the foodstuffs according to their effect on the body is the basis in order to achieve a harmonious status of health.

Dietary advisors do not recommend certain foodstuffs for everyone. The individual diet is tailor-made for the individual constitution.

Buy only fresh and ripe fruit and vegetables. You ought to leave unripe fruit and vegetables and such with brown spots and wilted leaves behind in the market. In this case take deep-frozen goods (never ready-to-serve dishes!). Fruit and vegetables are deep-frozen immediately after harvesting and often contain more vitamins and minerals than the goods from the vegetable shelf. Whereas conserved or tinned goods contain very much less biological substances. Also, salt, sugar and others are mostly added to the latter. Never leave the foodstuffs in the water after washing them to avoid that many vital substances get drowned. Clean salads, fruit and vegetables immediately before serving.

Please make sure of the hygienic processing of foodstuffs. Clean your salads, fruit and vegetables carefully. When cooking with meat, prepare all ingredients first and then process the meat products. Clean the worktop and tools very carefully. Wooden surfaces ought to be treated with a mild disinfectant regularly in order to reduce germination.
Store fruit and vegetables separately, if possible. Harvested fruit and vegetables are still alive and emit e.g. ethylene gas, which makes other products ripen and age faster. Keep meat and fish in the closed packaging or store them in the fridge in closed containers.

12.4 Herbs

There are some basic rules for storing medicinal herbs. On principle, herbs must be protected from direct sunlight, humidity and heat.

Containers for the storage of herbs may be glasses, ceramic jars and even plastic containers. However, plastic is a rather unsuitable material and should only be a short-term solution. In case of glass containers, use a dark material.

Medicinal herbs cannot be kept for any long period. The shelf life of herbs is limited. However, it can be prolonged with suitable storage. The place should be dark, rather cool and absolutely dry. A wooden medicine cabinet, placed not directly next to a source of heat, would be ideal. Never buy large quantities of herbs so as not to have to throw them away. Label the container with the name of the herb and the date of harvesting or processing.

13 Other dietic-books

The following syndromes of dietetics, TCM or for a therapy supplement for cancer are available.

Dietetics

E001. Nutrition of the infant - baby food
E002. Nutrition during lactation
E003. Nutrition in old age
E004. Nutrition of children and adolescents
E005. Nutrition of athletes
E006. Light weight
E007. Pregnancy
E008. Full food

Protein and electrolyte - kidneys
E009. (hemodialysis) dialysis treatment
E010. Acute renal failure
E011. Chronic renal insufficiency
E012. Nephrotic syndrome
E013. Kidney stones (nephrolithiasis)

Gastrointestinal tract - pancreas
E014. Acute pancreatitis (inflammation of the pancreas)
E015. Chronic pancreatitis (inflammation of the pancreas)

Gastrointestinal tract - small intestine and large intestine
E016. Acute obstipation (constipation)
E017. Chronic obstipation (constipation)
E018. Colon irritabile
E019. Diverticulitis
E020. Acquired lactose intolerance (lactose malabsorption)
E021. Fructose malabsorption
E022. Glutensensitive enteropathy (celiac disease)
E023. Colectomy
E024. Short Bowel Syndrome

Gastrointestinal tract - liver, gallbladder, bile ducts
E025. Acute and chronic hepatitis (inflammation of the liver)
E026. Cholelithiasis (bile stones)
E027. fatty liver
E028. cirrhosis

Gastrointestinal tract - Stomach and duodenal intestine
E029. Acute gastritis
E030. Chronic gastritis
E031. Stomach bleeding
E032. Ulcus ventriculi and duodenal ulcer
E033. Condition after gastric surgery

Gastrointestinal tract - oral cavity and esophagus
E034. Stomatitis
E035. Esophageal carcinoma (esophageal cancer)
E036. Refluosophagitis (heartburn)

Special diseases
E037. Phenylketonuria (PKU)
E038. Rheumatic joint diseases

Metabolism
E039. Obesity (overweight)
E040. Diabetes mellitus
E041. Eating disorders (underweight)

Fat metabolism
E042. Hypercholesterolaemia (increased cholesterol level)
E043. Hepatic Encephalopathy

Heart and circulation
E044. Arteriosclerosis (arterial calcification)
E045. Heart insufficiency
E046. Hypertension
E047. Hyperuricaemia and gout

Changed nutrient requirements
E048. In case of fever
E049. For malignant diseases
E050. After burns
E051. Radiation and chemotherapy

CANCER
E100. Pancreatic cancer
E101. Bladder cancer
E102. Blood cancer (leukemia)
E103. Breast cancer
E104. Colorectal cancer
E105. Gastric cancer
E106. Kidney cancer
E107. Esophageal cancer

TCM
E200. Bladder - moisture heat in the bladder
E201. Bladder - moisture and cold in the bladder
E202. Bladder - emptiness and cold in the bladder
E203. Large intestine - external cold affects the large intestine
E204. Large intestine - moisture heat in the large intestine
E205. Large intestine - heat blocks the intestine II acute
E206. Large intestine - dryness of the colon
E207. Large intestine - Yang deficiency (cold)
E208. Heart - Blood insufficiency
E209. Heart - Blood stagnation
E210. Heart - Fire
E211. Heart - Hot mucus clogs the heart pores

E212. Heart - Cold mucus clogs the heart pores
E213. Heart - Qi deficiency
E214. Heart - Yang deficiency
E215. Heart - Yin deficiency
E216. Liver - Ascending Liver Yang
E217. Liver - Blood deficiency
E218. Liver - Blood stagnation
E219. Liver - Moisture heat in liver and gall bladder
E220. Liver - Fire
E221. Liver - Gall bladder Qi-Empty
E222. Liver - Cold in the liver meridian
E223. Liver - Qi stagnation
E224. Liver - Wind
E225. Liver - Wind with ascending liver Yang
E226. Liver - Wind with blood anemic
E227. Liver - Wind with extreme heat
E228. Lung - Qi deficiency
E229. Lung - Mucus-moisture in the lungs
E230. Lung - Mucus-heat in the lungs
E231. Lung - Mucus-cold in the lungs
E232. Lung - Dryness of the lungs
E233. Lung - Wind-heat attacks the lungs
E234. Lung - Wind-cold affects the lungs
E235. Lung - Yin deficiency
E236. Stomach - Bloodstagnation
E237. Stomach - Fire
E238. Stomach - Cold with liquid
E239. Stomach - Nutrition stagnation
E240. Stomach - Qi deficiency
E241. Stomach - Rebellious Qi
E242. Stomach - Yin Emptiness
E243. Spleen - Heat and moisture attack the spleen
E244. Spleen - Coldness and moisture affects the spleen
E245. Spleen - Qi deficiency
E246. Spleen - Qi deficiency + Declining spleen Qi
E247. Spleen - Qi deficiency + spleen does not control the blood
E248. Spleen - Yang deficiency
E249. Kidney - Heart and kidney no longer communicate
E250. Kidney - Jing deficiency
E251. Kidney - Kidneys cannot receive the Qi
E252. Kidney - Qi is not stable
E253. Kidney - Yang deficiency
E254. Kidney - Yin deficiency

For further information visit di-book.com.